THE BRIDAL ROSE.

Once upon a time there lived a girl called Alexia who lived with her step-mother called Dora. Her step-mother was wicked and maltreated her because she had nobody to fight for her. She was all alone with her step-mother and had lost her father, mother, brother, sister and uncle in a wild forest of Uhanoba Kingdom.

Anytime she was maltreated she would run to the forest to cry. She would sing a song to her dead parents:

Mother! Mother!! Am all alone in

This world ever since you gave birth

To me. Oh! Oh!! Mother here I am

Alone...

Mother! Mother!! I have never been

Happy, I wish you were here with me

Oh! Oh!! Mama 2x

Oh! Sweet Mother I miss you.

One day a prince from another kingdom

took a stroll and headed to the forest for

hunting. He heard a singing sorrowful

voice like the whispers' of the spirit yet

beautiful to listen to. He took a pause and

listened to know where the voice was

coming from. He traced and finally met

her still singing. There he fell in love with

her because he could not have assumed

to meet with this kind of beautiful girl

with a thrilling voice of the gods and was

amazed.

He talked to her and they became friends.

They always met themselves at the forest

from time to time until her evil step-

mother found out.

Her step-mother lied to her that the

prince was deceiving her and at the same

time she was also telling the prince false

stories about Alexia

Dora was trying to create a disunity

between the two of them. And because

she had a black magic she knew about the

prophesy concerning Alexia which was the cause of Alexia's travails but Dora never knew that the gods were protecting her and that her actions will push her to her destiny.

Alexia was pregnant for her lover, prince Alex. Alexia told her step-mother to tell the prince that she was pregnant for him but her step-mother never did. Rather she was deceiving both of them as she told prince Alex that Alexia could never

be pregnant for him. Meanwhile she was

trying to find opportunity to kill the baby

inside Alexia with her black magic.

She could not harm the baby because the

baby was to fulfill the prophesy. She

however succeeded in making prince Alex

and Alexia hate themselves.

When it was time to give birth she went

through a lot of pains and she died but

the child was delivered a very, very

beautiful girl and was called Flora.

As time passed by the prince got married

and adopted a son and never knew about

the girl Alexia gave birth to. Some years passed and prince Alex became the king.

He later found out that before his lovely Alexia died she gave birth to a girl. So he decided to look for Flora his daughter.

But after searching for so long and could not find her he gave up. 15years passed and Flora was now a grown up girl and she always loved the forest just like her late mother.

But she was brain-washed by her grand step-mother that her father was evil.

When Flora was now a mature lady she was very beautiful and had many suitors but she had no interest in any of them even though she was a poor lady who lived and talked with animals.

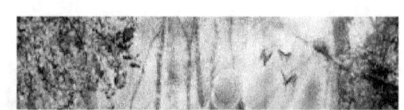

She often saw a castle and wished she lived there but, to her, it was impossible because she was poor.

The king was already very old and gave up all hope of seeing his daughter.

The king's adopted son Duncan just came back from a battle and had successfully conquered his enemies so they had a party and Flora wanted to attend the party. Since she was poor and dirty she sneaked into the palace and the adopted son Duncan saw her and arrested her. When the king heard about a girl sneaked in to his palace he was very curious and worried as he thought of his late beloved Alexia and as he could not find his daughter. He became mentally and emotionally disturbed. He became very harsh and strict with his words, thus making him a feared king. King Alex ordered that the girl should be detained

and put in chains. Prince Duncan feared

the harsh punishment and helped Flora

escape the palace castle.

Days, weeks and months passed by and one day Duncan saw Flora in the village and he recognized her. Duncan went to her and she knew him because she could not forget who saved her from the palace but ever since then she fell in love with Duncan and she could not hide her feelings. She told him she loved him and they continued to chat until it was dark in the evening and when the moon showed up they separated and said good bye to themselves.

When the prince got home to sleep at night on his bed he was dreaming. He saw Flora in a castle wearing a black gown on their wedding but was confused and his heart quivered fast. The whole place was dark with mystical steps and a solo sounds. The prince got up and was afraid because he immediately got a trance on Flora as the daughter of his forester father that they have been searching for.

He got up with courage and this was in the morning to see the palace sorcerer and spiritual adviser by name Zoo-Marina. She was a white witch.

He narrated his dream to Zoo-Marina.

And Zoo-Marina had to perform some mystical works by going into the spirit world for guidance.

Before Zoo-Marina came back from the

spirit world the prince (Duncan) had

already left to see Flora his love. When he

got to Flora's home he knocked at the

door. He got a reply but not the voice of

Flora.

"Who is at the door?" asked Dora.

"I am Prince Duncan," replied the prince.

She quickly transformed into a very beautiful lady and opened the door. When Duncan beheld Dora he began to admire her as he had been mesmerized by her seductive and bewitched appearance.

Dora already knew that Flora was about to come in. She quickly cast a spell on Duncan to forget her appearance and how she was trying to seduce him.

Shortly thereafter Dora left the prince and Flora.

The prince focused deeply at the face of Flora and immediately proposed to her. Flora had her head downcast for some moments. When she raised her head tears streamed down her eyes and the prince moved closer to her and as he held her close to himself she muttered a few words into his ears: "I love you. I accept your proposal. But, I wonder if the king your father would accept me as his daughter-in-law, for I am poor and have no parents nor relations to call my own and to plead my cause." The prince responded, "I shall be there for you as father, mother, brother and everything that shall give you warmth and care. My father shall be there as your father. My father the king has a heart of gold, if understood."

They were very happy with themselves.

The happiness was more on the prince because he was deeply in love with her.

So he happily went to tell his father.

At the time prince Duncan was telling the king about his proposal and how far he had gone on it the white witch came in with her findings telling the king of his long-lost daughter and that he will live to see his lost daughter before he will pass on.

She also said that she was seeing chaos and a dark kingdom but that the king should take precautions on his decision on the day of the prince's wedding. She added that only the act of true love will bring peace to save his kingdom. She also said that after seven moons there will be a ceremony on the 18th day of the seventh month. On the day of the ceremony there shall be 18 young ladies of nubile age. They shall all be dressed in white gowns. One of these shall appear

as though she had a black gown on

whereas she is like others wearing a

white gown. This one is your daughter

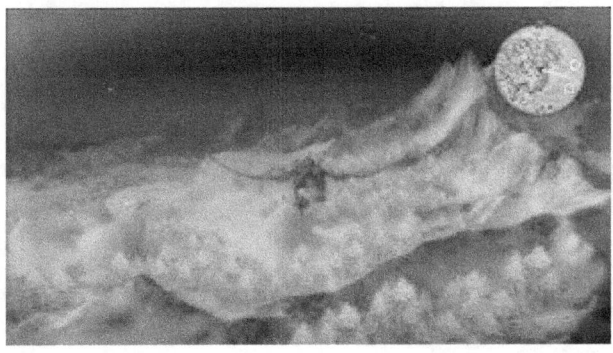

This gave the king some deep thought.

This signified terror and an un-united kingdom. With all of this the king was bothered and was in a deep sea.

Seven moons passed by and the preparation for the prince's wedding started. On that day the king was dressed in his attire. Everybody was very happy to see their prince getting married but the grand-step mother of Flora wasn't happy at all because this wedding will ruin her and her quest to take-over the kingdom.

So she performed some black magic because this was her final chance to fulfill her wish. She made some incantations to change the wedding gown to black in order for her spells to work in destroying the kingdom.

So the ceremony began and all the people were seeing the ladies all dressed in white gowns. But the king and the prince saw the 18th lady in a poor white gown appearing black and a changed face not looking like Flora. The king and the

prince chose this 18th person.

As she was stepping forward to the alter

everybody including the prince were all

afraid as they saw her in a black gown.

There the king her father quickly figured

out the parable of Zoo-Marina about the

18th number. The number 18 stands for

18years of his lost daughter who had

grown to become 18 years in age.

 He quickly ordered the crowed to silence

and he burst into tears and ran towards

his daughter and said to everyone there

that the ceremony is on till the following

day but the marriage will be on the third

day that he has found his lost daughter

the celebration continued.....

Flora was both sad and full of joy.

She immediately expressed shock and in

mixed reaction she coldly voiced to the

king: "Oh no, oh no, no you couldn't have

been my father. You can't be my father.

This can't be happening. I have suffered

for too long without a father and without

a mother. What is my crime?" She cried in tears remembering the past. The king told Flora how he searched for her and how much he missed his beloved Alexia, her mother.

It came as if the wind was blowing in rush and snows started falling. This was the expression of the gods in their happiness because for 18 years there have been difficulties in the land. As the wind blew the gown was blown away from her body.

The strength of Flora's feelings could not be comprehended by the evils that surrounded the kingdom before now. All evils were gone with the wind and in turn the spell started to shatter like a snow melting under the intense heat of the sun.

So three days after the ceremony continued. She was very full of life seeing the people rejoicing with the king and her. On the third day they got married and the rain fell to water the crops of the

farmers. And they lived happily ever

after.

The black witch eventually died and was

thrown into the sea as food for the fishes.

The villagers now made that day a

memorable day for celebration every

year as this was the cause of good

fortune to the kingdom.

www.ingramcontent.com/pod-product-compliance
Lightning Source LLC
Chambersburg PA
CBHW060350290526
45791CB00004B/1616